# HARRY HOUDINI
# MASTER of MAGIC

# HARRY HOUDINI
## MASTER of MAGIC

## by ROBERT KRASKE

### Cover by Bob Clark

SCHOLASTIC INC.
New York Toronto London Auckland Sydney Tokyo

# For Bruce Clarke

Photo credits: *The Original Houdini Scrapbook* by Walter B. Gibson © 1976 by Sterling Publishing Co., Inc., pages 18, 27, 64 top, 67; courtesy Milbourne Christopher, pages 20, 42, 49, 69; Bettmann Archive, page 40; UPI, pages 53, 54, 64 bottom; Theatre and Music Collection, The Museum of the City of New York, page 56.

ISBN 0-590-05374-4

18 17 16 15 14 13 12 11 10 9 8 7        4 5 6 7 8 9/8

# Contents

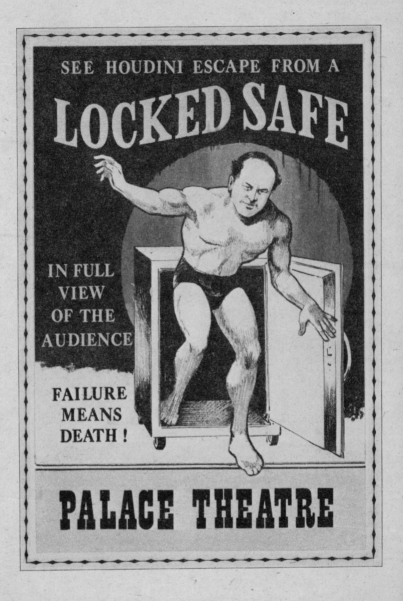

# 1. The Great Houdini

The new safe stood on the stage of the Euston Palace Theatre in London. Its door was swung wide open. Harry Houdini, the young American magician, got ready to step inside. He was wearing only a bathing suit.

London newspapers had printed these bold headlines: "Houdini Challenges Safe Maker. Offers to Escape from Safe Before Theatre Audience." The year was 1904.

The people watching from the audience were excited. "The air in the safe will last only a few minutes," one man said.

"He'll die if he doesn't get out fast!"

"It's impossible! How could anyone escape from a locked safe?"

"Houdini can!"

On the stage Houdini shook hands with men

who had come up from the audience. They had looked over the safe to make sure it was in good working order. A doctor had examined Houdini. He had even asked the magician to open his mouth. "No tools!" he told the audience. "Nothing on him!"

"Then," Houdini said, shaking hands with the last man, "let me enter the safe. Lock the door behind me!"

The heavy steel door clanged shut. A screen was placed around the safe. As the men left the stage, the orchestra played soft music. The audience settled back in their seats to wait. They watched the screen.

A half hour passed. The people began to grow restless.

"How can he possibly get out?" a woman asked.

One man thought he knew the answer. "Houdini isn't like the rest of us," he whispered. "He has supernatural powers! He can change himself into a spirit and slip between the cracks of the door — just like smoke!"

The woman looked at him. "I don't believe that!"

"Believe me," the man said, turning away. "It's true!"

Forty minutes passed. "Open the door!" someone yelled. "He's dead and can't get out!" A woman screamed and fainted.

Forty-five minutes. People were whistling and stamping. A man stood and shook his fist. "Let him out! He needs help!"

At that moment, Houdini stepped from behind the screen. A great sigh swept through the audience.

"There he is!"

"He's alive!"

Men rushed onto the stage to inspect the safe. "The door is locked!"

Houdini smiled and bowed to the cheering people.

How had he escaped from a steel safe? No one in the audience that night guessed the answer. The fact was that Houdini had escaped in just fourteen minutes. He had been sitting behind the screen for almost a half hour while the audience's excitement grew.

Many years ago, before movies, radio, or TV, Harry Houdini was the greatest magician and escape artist in the world. Some people thought he was born with magical powers. But this was not true. He became a master magician only after long years of hard work. In fact, he began working toward this goal when he was a boy.

Houdini's real name was Ehrich Weiss. He was born in Budapest, Hungary, in 1874, the third of five children of Mayer Samuel and Cecilia Weiss. Shortly after Ehrich's birth, Samuel Weiss brought his family to America. They made their home in Appleton, Wisconsin.

Samuel Weiss was a rabbi, the religious leader of the Jewish people in Appleton. His congregation was small and couldn't pay Rabbi Weiss enough to support his wife and children. As they grew up, Ehrich and his brothers had to earn money for the family by shining shoes and selling newspapers.

When Ehrich wasn't working or going to school,

he practiced doing tricks. At the age of nine, he hung ropes from a tree branch in his backyard. Then he tied a wooden bar to the ropes. He learned to do such good stunts on the homemade trapeze that one of his friends asked him to be in his five-cent circus. Feeling like a real circus star, Ehrich called himself "The Prince of the Air." He loved the clapping and cheering of the boys and girls who watched him.

He also practiced rope escapes. He put his hands behind his back and let friends tie his wrists together with a rope. After a few minutes, he held up the rope. His friends were all amazed! How had he escaped? Ehrich only smiled. He had already learned the first rule of being a magician: Never tell how you do a trick!

Mother Weiss was amazed at another trick her son had learned. Pieces of her apple cake began to disappear, so she hid the cake in a cupboard and locked the door. The cake still vanished. One day, after several cakes had disappeared, she found out where they went. Her son had a new interest —

picking locks. The small lock on her cupboard door was easy to open with a bent piece of wire.

"That doesn't surprise me!" the town locksmith said. He had heard about Ehrich's trick. "That boy has been coming to my shop for weeks. He can pick any lock in the place!"

In 1887, when Ehrich was thirteen, Rabbi Weiss moved his family to New York. There were more Jewish people there, and Rabbi Weiss hoped to start a small religious school. But he became ill and could do nothing to support his wife and five children.

To help his sick father, Ehrich took whatever jobs he could find. During one Christmas season, he worked as a package delivery boy for a large store. One day he lettered a card and pinned it to his hat:

Christmas is coming;
Turkeys are fat.
Please drop a quarter
In the Messenger Boy's hat.

That evening he stood in front of his mother. "Shake me," he said. "I'm magic!" As she shook her son, Mrs. Weiss's eyes opened wide. Quarters dropped out of her son's sleeves and fell into her lap.

"Ehrich!" she exclaimed in German, the language that she always spoke. "There's enough money to pay the rent this week!" She hugged her hardworking son.

After Christmas Ehrich looked for another job. As he walked along Broadway, he came upon a line of boys in front of a small factory — H. Richter's Sons. A sign in the window read: "Assistant necktie cutter wanted."

Ehrich was only fourteen years old, but he boldly walked to the head of the line. He took the sign off the door. "The job is taken," he told the boys. "Thank you for waiting." His bluff worked. He got the job and stayed at H. Richter's Sons for the next two and a half years.

During these years Ehrich practiced magic in his spare time. He did card tricks and trick rope ties. He read books on magic and gave magic shows in neighborhood clubs. He called himself "Cardo" or "Eric the Great."

These clubs paid Ehrich a few dollars for each show. Mother Weiss was always waiting for the extra money — to buy medicine for Papa who was sick in bed, to put food on the table, and to pay the rent. The money helped, but magic was only a hobby. Ehrich never thought about making a living doing tricks.

## 2. "Behold! A Miracle!"

One day when Ehrich was sixteen, he went into a bookstore. Looking along the shelves, he came across an old book on the life of Robert-Houdin. It was a moment that changed his life.

Jean Eugène Robert-Houdin was the greatest magician in France. He performed before the French emperor and before England's Queen Victoria. He pulled cannonballs from an empty hat. He made trees grow fruit on the stage. He even floated ladies in midair.

Ehrich spent the night reading Robert-Houdin's life story. The next morning his mother found him in bed still reading.

"Ehrich!" she scolded. "So much reading! It will hurt your eyes!"

"Mother!" Ehrich said "Please! Never mind my

eyes. I am reading the most important book of my life!"

"So!" Mother Weiss said. "What makes this book so important at six o'clock in the morning?"

Ehrich held up the book. "This man — Robert-Houdin — has made me see that I can make magic my life's work. If he did it, so can I!"

Mother Weiss's eyebrows lifted. "A fine thought, Ehrich. But can you make money doing magic? Remember poor Papa. He is unable to work for us. There's the rent to pay, and we must eat."

Ehrich stared at the book. "I don't know how much money I can make. But I want to become a magician — just like Robert-Houdin!"

Within a few days Ehrich left his job at H. Richter's Sons. He also made another important change. To honor his hero, he decided to change his name to "Houdini." Since friends called him "Ehrie," which sounded like "Harry," he became "Harry Houdini." He was seventeen years old.

Harry's younger brother, Theo, was also interested in magic, so they decided to become partners. Mother Weiss sewed satin costumes —

jackets and short pants — for her two sons, and they began practicing tricks together. Calling themselves "The Houdini Brothers," they gave shows wherever they could — at neighborhood parties, club meetings, and beer halls. The pay was small, but they were learning how to be magicians.

Their show was simple and fast moving. Harry touched the buttonhole of his jacket, and a flower appeared. He reached into a candle flame and pulled out a red handkerchief. He did card tricks. Then came the big trick of the show!

The audience watched as Harry tied Theo's hands behind his back. Theo then stepped into a trunk. Harry closed the lid and locked it. After tying a rope around the trunk, he placed a screen in front of it.

Harry stepped to the front of the stage. "When I clap my hands three times — behold! A miracle!"

He clapped his hands and then stepped behind the screen. A moment later Theo stepped in front of the screen. Setting the screen to one side, Theo untied the trunk. He lifted the lid, and Harry stepped out. His hands were tied behind his back.

**Young Houdini gives a magic show.**

Harry had purchased the trunk from another magician. It had a board on one side that was loose and opened into the trunk. Both Theo and Harry slipped through the opening and left the rope and lock untouched. The audience, of course, didn't know about the loose board. Harry and Theo had practiced the trick until they could slip in and out in seconds.

After one show, when Harry and Theo returned to the Weiss apartment, they found their mother in tears. "Your father!" she gasped. "Go to him!"

In the bedroom they found that Rabbi Weiss was dying. The old man made Harry swear on the Bible always to care for his mother.

Slowly the name of The Houdini Brothers became known. Two years after Harry and Theo started their act, they went to the 1893 Chicago World's Fair. They performed their act on an outdoor stage set up with others along a midway. People walked past the stages, stopping here and there to watch the sword swallower, the fire eater, the strong man, or the jugglers, and perhaps the Houdinis.

The next year Harry and Theo took their act to Coney Island in New York. At the end of one performance, the show manager, Sam Gumpertz, called Harry aside. "Harry, you shouldn't say, 'You

**Harry and Bess Houdini with their trick
escape trunk.**

can see I ain't got nothin' up my sleeve.' "

Harry was surprised. "What's wrong with it?"

But once Harry understood that good English would help his act, he worked hard to improve his grammar.

While he worked at Coney Island, an important event happened in Harry's life. He got married.

The girl's full name was Wilhelmina Beatrice Rahner, but she was called "Bess." She was tiny and had dark hair. On the day of their marriage, they had known each other for only ten days. Bess was eighteen, and Harry was nineteen.

For The Houdini Brothers' magic act, the marriage came at the right time. Theo was growing too big to squeeze in and out of the escape trunk. Bess weighed only 94 pounds. She could easily slip through the open board. So Bess joined Harry in the act, and Theo went off to start a new act of his own.

Bess and Harry called themselves the "Master Monarchs of Modern Mystery." They were young. They were sure of themselves. They would get ahead in life — by magic. Or so they thought.

# 3. Dime Museum Harry

"Bess," Harry said one day, "we have a good act. We're ready to play the big theaters in New York!"

But the theater owners didn't agree. Morning after morning Bess and Harry left Mother Weiss's apartment and went to the theaters. On a half-dark stage, they went through their magic act. The owners, sitting amid rows of empty seats, watched with little interest. They saw Bess as a thin little girl in a shabby costume. The suit Harry wore was wrinkled and the pants baggy.

"Your act," one of the theater owners said, "may be okay for Coney Island or the midway at the World's Fair. But New York is the top — the big time — see? You have to be something special to play these theaters." He placed a hand on Harry's shoulder. "There are dozens of magic acts better than yours. Sorry, kids."

Harry was hurt. "What's the matter with those guys?" he said to Bess outside the theater. "Can't they tell we're good?" Then his spirits lifted, as they always did no matter how often the theater owners said "no." "Who needs 'em!" He placed an arm around Bess. "One of these days they'll be begging us to work on their stages! Just wait!"

Bess smiled up at her confident husband. "In the meantime, let's try a dime museum!"

"Why not!" Harry said. "They know a good act when they see one!"

In the 1890s, there were dime museums in many American towns. For ten cents each, people could walk along a line of small stages and watch different kinds of shows. They might see the strong man lift heavy weights. At the next stage, they could watch a man slide a sword down his throat. Then they might come upon a fire eater placing a burning stick into his mouth. They could also look at Siamese twins, bearded ladies, dwarfs, giants, and a magician or two.

In those dime museums in and around New York and in the Midwest, Harry and Bess gave six to twenty shows a day. Harry did card tricks. He changed the color of a silk handkerchief by pushing it through an empty paper tube. He yanked two knotted pieces of rope through his neck and escaped from handcuffs. But it didn't seem to matter how hard he worked. People weren't impressed with his tricks. They clapped politely, then moved on to the next show.

"Humph!" Harry snorted. "Some people don't know how good we are!"

The next year Bess and Harry joined the Welsh Brothers' Circus in Pennsylvania. They gave their show on a small stage for a salary of $25 per week. To make extra money, Bess walked among the people in the audience and sold "trick" decks of cards. Harry sold toothpaste and soap to the other circus people. They needed the extra money. Each week Harry sent half of his salary to his mother in New York. He hadn't forgotten the promise he had made to his father.

Traveling with the circus was hard, but it often gave Harry a chance to learn new tricks. An old Japanese acrobat showed him how to swallow objects, hold them in his throat, then use his throat muscles to bring them up again. The old man would pop an ivory ball into his mouth. When he opened his mouth wide, it was empty. Then — presto! — he would take the ball from between his lips.

Each day the old man watched as Harry practiced. He used a small peeled potato at the end of a string, so that it could be pulled back when necessary. Within a few weeks, when his throat muscles had become strong enough, Harry was swallowing ivory balls and bringing them back up easily. It was a valuable trick to know. He would use it in the future to hide tools for his escape acts.

During these months with the circus, Harry became more and more interested in locks. Wherever the circus went, he visited locksmith shops. He studied locks and took them apart to find out how they worked. He found that most door locks — and handcuffs too — were easy to open. Some could be opened with a sharp rap as easily as with a key. For others he used a steel pick, a tiny wire, a watch spring, even a piece of string. At night he read books on locks. Whenever Harry could spare some money, he bought a pair of handcuffs. Soon he had a large collection.

Harry and Bess enjoyed working in the circus, but the season was soon over, and they had to look for another job. Even though Harry had sent money to his mother faithfully every week, he had managed to save a little money. With this sum he now bought a part interest in a traveling show. He and Bess did their act, and Harry helped manage the show.

Harry tried to interest theater owners in the show by getting stories about his act in the newspapers. His first stories appeared in newspapers that winter. In two Massachusetts towns, Harry visited the police station and invited policemen to handcuff him. As newspaper reporters watched, he stepped into a closet. In a few moments, he stepped out with the cuffs off.

"Has No Use for Handcuffs," one paper reported. "Houdini Surprises Police," another newspaper wrote.

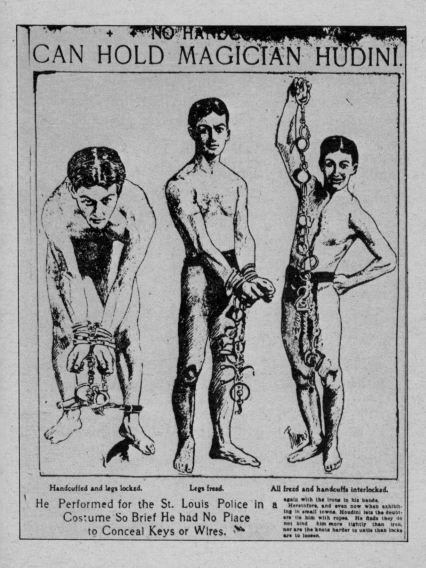

# CAN HOLD MAGICIAN HUDINI.

**+ + NO HAND**

Handcuffed and legs locked.

Legs freed.

All freed and handcuffs interlocked.

He Performed for the St. Louis Police in a Costume So Brief He had No Place to Conceal Keys or Wires.

again with the irons in his hands.

Heretofore, and even now when exhibiting in small towns, Houdini lets the doubters tie him with ropes. He finds they do not bind him more tightly than iron, nor are the knots harder to untie than locks are to loosen.

Despite Harry's newspaper stories, the traveling show failed, and Harry and Bess were once more looking for work. Harry still felt that theater owners would be more interested in hiring him if they had read about his act first. He tried to think of new stunts that would make newspapers write about him. Sometimes these stunts didn't work out as he planned.

In one town he told reporters that he would do a special escape trick. "Gentlemen," he said, "I intend to escape from handcuffs while tied to a horse."

The stunt took place on a dirt road on the edge of town. Harry asked one reporter to handcuff his wrists in front of him. He gave a piece of rope to another reporter and asked him to tie his ankles under the horse's stomach.

"Now watch carefully," Harry said. "As this good horse walks around the field, I will free myself from these bonds!"

But the horse had other ideas. As Harry began to twist and turn, trying to free himself, the horse became startled and took off. Across fields and over fences the frightened animal ran with the young magician clinging to its mane.

Miles away from town, the horse finally stopped. Harry took off the cuffs, untied his ankles, and slid painfully to the ground. He had performed the trick — but there was no one around to watch.

Harry and Bess drifted out to the Midwest where their luck had always been good. They worked for a week now and then, but mostly theater owners said, "Sorry, I can't use you." To Bess especially, it seemed as if they were constantly packing and unpacking their trunks and moving from city to city.

# 4. Talking with the Spirits of the Dead

The next fall Bess and Harry were still traveling, working a week now and then in small town theaters. In Kansas they joined Dr. Hill's California Concert Company. Dr. Hill was a large man with a flowing beard. He sold bottles of medicine to people in small towns. His medicine, he said, cured back pain, falling hair, and ingrown toenails. People didn't know that he mixed the medicine himself.

To gather a crowd of people to buy his medicine, Dr. Hill gave shows. For $25 a week, he hired Harry and Bess to do their magic act. After their act, they changed costumes and, with other members of the company, put on a play. When the play was over, Dr. Hill came on stage. He told the people about his wonderful medicine and sold it for one dollar a bottle.

As winter came, audiences for Dr. Hill's shows grew smaller. He could hardly pay his actors. One evening he called Harry to his hotel room. "Now that winter is here, we have to do something about getting more people to see our shows. I know just the thing that will bring them in." He put an arm around Harry's shoulders. "We'll give 'em a seance, and you'll be the spiritualist — you know, talkin' with spooks and giving out messages from dead relatives. Just stick with me, and I'll show you how to do it."

He held up a sign. "How do you like it? It's going on the front of the theater tomorrow."

Lettered in bold print were the words: "Tonight! Eight o'clock! Houdini the Great will hold a seance! See him — hear him — talk with spirits of the dead!"

Early in the morning, Harry went with Dr. Hill to visit the town graveyard. From gravestones, they wrote down the names of dead people and the dates they died.

"Now we're going to see Mr. Potter," Dr. Hill said. "He's lived here all his life."

For five dollars, Mr. Potter told Dr. Hill about people in the town and about their family problems. Harry listened carefully.

That night the theater was jammed. Harry walked to the center of the stage. "I need three men on stage with me. Who will come forward?"

Three men came up the steps at the side of the stage. Harry told them to tie him to a chair. In front of him they placed a screen. Then they went back to their seats. In fifteen minutes they were to come back and remove the screen. The audience settled back to wait.

Soon, from behind the screen, bells rang and a banjo plinked. A ghostly form floated above the screen. Then there was silence.

The same three men went back on the stage. They took away the screen. Harry was still tied to the chair.

The people were amazed. Spirits and ghosts must have made those sounds! They had actually seen a ghost above the screen!

They didn't know, of course, that Harry had slipped out of the rope—rope escapes were easy for him. He had rung the bell and plinked the banjo, then hidden them out of sight through the stage curtain behind him.

To make the "ghost" float over the screen, he had used a short rod that opened to the length of a fishpole. He placed a white sheet on the pole and lifted it above the screen. In the dim light of the stage, it looked just like a ghost. Then he retied his hands and waited for the men to untie him.

After seeing these wonders, the people were willing to believe that the young magician was indeed in touch with spirits.

Stepping to the front of the stage, Harry said, "Ladies and gentlemen, may I have complete quiet!" He closed his eyes. "I — I feel strange beings!" He placed a hand on his forehead. "I feel a message coming through!"

The people looked at one another. Who would get a message from the spirits?

"Is there—someone here tonight—named Fred Merkle?"

A man jumped to his feet. "I'm Fred Merkle," he croaked.

Harry pretended that the message from the spirits was coming through slowly. "I have a message — from your dear departed mother, Emma. 'Do not — do not sell the farm yet, dear Freddie! A better offer will come!' "

Fred Merkle sat down, stunned. Houdini the Great was right! He had been thinking about selling the farm. His mother's first name was Emma. And she had always called him "Freddie." Houdini was truly in touch with the spirit of his dead mother!

And so the seance went. The people in the audience heard names, dates, and family secrets. "How could Houdini know all these things about us," they said, "unless the spirits told him?"

Harry enjoyed the attention that people gave him now. As he walked down the main street of town with Bess, people pointed to him. Women nodded, and men tipped their hats.

Harry and Bess traveled with Dr. Hill's show through the Midwest and into Canada. Sometimes Houdini gave out messages from "spirits" about future events. One of these messages turned out to be true, although it was just a guess on Harry's part.

Coming into one town, Houdini saw a mother scolding her son. The boy had been riding his bicycle carelessly in the street.

That night Houdini told the people in the theater that he had a message for Ella Jenkins, the boy's mother. Closing his eyes, he said:

"I see a boy speeding down a hill on a bicycle. He is trying to turn a corner! Watch out! He has crashed! He is bloody. I see an arm hanging limply."

The next night the mother came again to the theater. She told the surprised magician and the audience that her son had fallen from his bicycle and broken his arm that very afternoon!

After this, people believed even more firmly that Houdini could look into the future. But Houdini began to feel uncomfortable, and so did Bess. They felt that card tricks and handcuff escapes were good entertainment. People knew they were being fooled, and they enjoyed it. But setting out to make people believe something untrue — making them think he could see into the future and talk to people's dead relatives — was less than honest.

After the boy broke his arm, Houdini felt that people were beginning to believe too much in his spirit powers. "I don't like it," he told Bess. "It's time to quit giving seances."

Bess agreed. After six months, he and Bess left Dr. Hill and headed for Mother Weiss's apartment in New York.

# 5. The Handcuff King

Mother Weiss had a sure cure for colds, stomachaches, and gloomy feelings—hot chicken soup. Harry needed plenty of his mother's soup. He was unhappy. For seven years he had been a performer, and he still had not become famous. Theater owners in New York thought of him as "Dime Museum Harry" and would not hire him.

"I don't know what to do," he told Bess. "Maybe we'll give up the magic show."

To earn money, he wrote a sixteen-page book called *Magic Made Easy*. Few people bought it. Next, he went to four newspapers and offered to sell his handcuff secrets for $20. No one was interested. More weeks went by, and Harry could not get a job. Finally he told Bess, "Let's try traveling again. If we're not successful after one more year,

I'll get a regular job. I'll make a wonderful locksmith!" Bess, ever faithful, agreed.

They joined the Welsh Brothers' Circus again and spent the summer traveling through the Midwest. In the fall they played in a dime museum in Chicago and several theaters in small towns. Then they went home to New York and more dime museums.

They gave as many as 20 shows a day. Harry did a watch disappearing trick and card tricks. He turned a silk handkerchief into a live pigeon. He challenged people to snap handcuffs on his wrists, and he escaped from them right before their eyes. He and Bess ended each show with the trunk escape.

"What's wrong with us, Bess?" Harry said one day when the year was almost up. "Don't we put on a good show? Why do people clap a little and then move on? Why aren't they cheering?" His shoulders slumped, and he shoved his hands deep into his pockets.

Bess slipped a hand through his arm. "We just need a break — some good luck."

Once or twice a week, between shows, Harry called on theater owners. But to them he was still "Dime Museum Harry." They refused to watch his act. After a while, he stopped going to the theaters. Then, unexpectedly, something happened.

One spring evening Harry and Bess had finished their last show. A short, red-faced man they'd never seen before came up to their stage and invited them to dinner.

"Kid," he said bluntly, "you're a rotten showman!" Harry's jaw grew hard. "Now take it easy and listen to me. You're trying to do too much — giving a 30-minute act in 10 minutes. But you do one thing that's really different—your challenge to people in the audience to lock you up with handcuffs. That's good! I'll try you out at $60 per week. My name is Martin Beck."

Harry's mouth opened. Martin Beck! The manager of the Orpheum Circuit, the largest chain of theaters in the West! Harry shook the man's hand eagerly.

In a theater in Omaha the next week, Harry knew that he would not race through his tricks.

Harry Handcuff Houdini.

Dressed in a well-fitted new suit, he calmly walked on stage. "I would like to invite any members of the audience who have brought handcuffs or leg irons to step forward and test me."

Martin Beck had asked two policemen to bring cuffs to the theater. Now they stepped onto the stage. They snapped five pairs of handcuffs on Harry's wrists and arms and a set of irons on his ankles. Then Harry stepped into a curtained cabinet in the center of the stage. The band played. In a few minutes Houdini stepped out of the cabinet. His clothes were wrinkled, and he was perspiring. He held the irons and handcuffs up to the audience. Then he and Bess ended the act with the trunk escape.

As the curtain came down, the audience cheered. "Bess! Bess!" Harry cried. "Do you hear that! They're cheering for me! For us!"

Martin Beck was as pleased as the audience. "It's not how many tricks you do," he said, "it's how you do them!" He hired Houdini for his theater in San Francisco and raised his pay to $90 per week.

In San Francisco Harry called newspaper reporters to his hotel room. He told them that he would ask policemen in the San Francisco Police Department to lock him in handcuffs so he couldn't escape.

The next day he went to police headquarters. Police doctors told Harry to take off his clothes so they could look for tools. They looked in his mouth, ears, nose, and hair. When they could find none, policemen handcuffed his hands behind his back. Then they locked irons on his ankles and placed a chain of handcuffs between his wrists and ankles. The policemen grinned at Houdini. They were only too glad to make a fool of the young magician. They picked him up, carried him into a closet, and locked the door.

Ten minutes later Harry stepped out of the closet and dropped the irons to the floor.

The next day a San Francisco newspaper carried a half-page story about Houdini's escape. Harry was thrilled — his first big newspaper story!

In each new city, Harry performed first for police officials. Reporters were always present. Houdini's escapes always made good stories for their readers.

Now Beck sent him to Kansas City. He escaped in eight minutes from a cell at Central Police Station. A newspaper called him the "Champion Jail

Breaker." What the paper didn't know was that Harry had planned his escape in advance. Before offering to escape from a jail, he always called on the sheriff. The sheriff was pleased to receive his visit and willing to show him around. This gave Harry a chance to look at the locks on the cells. Sometimes, when the sheriff wasn't watching, he fastened a wire pick under a lock with wax. At other times, he managed to take a wax mold of a key. Later he made a second key.

People wanted to believe that Houdini really was magic. But the truth of his escapes was something else. There was no magic in them, only hard work and constant practice.

He never stopped working. Every morning he did exercises to build his strength. He even practiced to keep his fingers nimble. While talking with people, he would take a half-dollar from his pocket and roll it across his knuckles. Or he would take a string, tie it in several knogs, and drop it on the floor. Slipping off his shoes and socks, he would untie and retie the knots with his toes.

One year had passed since his talk with Martin Beck. Beck had helped him become a stage star in the West and Midwest, but he couldn't help Houdini in New York City. "I don't manage any of the big theaters there," he told Harry.

Harry shook hands with the short, pudgy man. "You gave me my start," he said. "I'll always be grateful to you."

In New York Harry still could not get a job in a big theater. So he decided to do what other show people had done—go to Europe. If he could make a name for himself in London, Paris, and Berlin, he knew the New York theater owners would fight to hire him.

One day in late May 1900, Harry and Bess said good-bye to Mother Weiss and boarded a ship for Europe.

There were only two problems: They didn't know anyone in Europe, and no one there had heard of The Great Houdini.

# 6. A Big Hit in Europe

When Harry and Bess arrived in London, Harry immediately started to look for a theater owner who would hire him. At the Alhambra Theatre, he showed the manager, Dundas Slater, a scrapbook of newspaper stories about himself.

"You say you're good," Slater said. "Well, we'll see. I'll hire you—but only if you can get out of the cuffs at Scotland Yard."

"Fair enough!" Harry said. "You get the reporters to come with me, and I'll go this afternoon."

At police headquarters — Scotland Yard — that afternoon, Superintendent Melville was glad to show how his English-made handcuffs could hold the young American magician.

"Place your arms around this marble pillar," he told Harry. Then he snapped the cuffs on Harry's wrists. "There now! That should hold you. Come on, lads," he said to the reporters. "We'll come back in an hour or so and let him loose!"

The men turned to leave.

"Better take your cuffs with you, Superintendent!" Harry called as Melville opened the door. He handed the open cuffs to the amazed police superintendent.

Newspapers published the story, and news of Houdini's escape quickly spread around London. Dundas Slater hired him for two weeks at $300 per week. But so many people came to the theater that Houdini stayed for six months.

The English were delighted to test their handcuffs and irons on Houdini. In December two sailors from H.M.S. *Powerful* brought British navy irons to the theater. Houdini sat on the stage, knees tucked up to his chin. The sailors placed a broom handle under his knees and over the bend of his elbows. Then they bound him with chains and locks. A screen was placed around him. When Houdini escaped in seconds, the British audience cheered and cheered.

From London Houdini and Bess went to Germany. To get German newspapers to write stories about him, he gave a public show. Locked into cuffs, irons, and chains, he jumped off a bridge and freed himself underwater. When he climbed up the riverbank, a policeman arrested him —for walking on the grass! People laughed when they read the story in their papers.

In Berlin carpenters challenged Houdini to escape from a packing box. Houdini lay down in the box, and the carpenters nailed the lid on. A screen was placed around the box. An orchestra played a loud march. In a few minutes Houdini stepped from behind the screen. The carpenters rushed back on stage to inspect the box. They found the lid still firmly in place!

Houdini became the best-known showman in Germany. During the next four years, he and Bess traveled throughout Europe. Wherever he went, newspapers wrote stories about him, and people crowded into theaters to see him.

Back in London, his fans saw him perform his greatest escape—from a steel safe on the stage of the Euston Palace Theatre.

Houdini, wearing heavy chains and a bathing suit, is ready to jump in the water.

His escape was really simple, so simple that no one guessed how he did it.

When the men from the audience came onto the stage to look over the safe, it was a part of Houdini's escape plan. After the doctor had examined him and had told the audience that he had no tools, Harry shook hands with all the men on the stage. The last man was a friend. He had a tiny screwdriver under a ring. Harry "palmed" the tool and stepped into the safe.

Inside, he used the screwdriver to remove screws holding a plate over the lock on the inside of the door. Then he was able to open the door from the inside. He stepped out, screwed the plate back in place, and closed the door.

After London Harry and Bess went to Scotland. In July 1905 they decided to return home. Harry missed his mother. He wanted desperately to see her again. Besides, he had done what he came to do. He was Europe's best-known showman. He was earning $1,200 per week.

The audience clapped and cheered as Harry left the theater after his last performance. He placed

Bess in a horse-drawn cab with their trunks. Then a group of young men lifted him to their shoulders and jogged to the train station, singing, "And when ye go, will ye nae come back?"

He had made sure reporters were there to write about his leave-taking. It would be another story for New York theater owners to read and learn that, in Europe, he had been a big hit. No longer would they dare to call him "Dime Museum Harry"!

# 7. The Man Who Walked Through Walls

Houdini and Bess returned to New York to a new home at 278 West 113th Street.

"Ehrich!" Mother Weiss said. "What will you do with all these rooms?"

The new house was four stories high and had 26 rooms. Harry lifted his mother and swung her around the room. "One of them is just for you. I'm moving you out of your apartment today!"

Houdini was like a child with a new toy. He filled several rooms with books on magic. In the basement were crates of magic tricks and hundreds of locks, leg irons, chains, and keys.

New York theater owners gave him little time to fix up his house. His success in Europe had made him famous, and they all wanted to hire him for their theaters.

Theater owners in other cities also wanted him.

**Houdini escapes from a straitjacket while hanging upside-down.**

In Washington he escaped from a giant paper bag — made from a single sheet of paper — without tearing it. In Philadelphia a college football team used a brass chain to tie him into a giant football. He was out in 35 minutes.

He escaped from whatever people could think

up—a cube of clear glass, a U.S. government mail bag, and even a large sausage skin. Six iron workers in Boston sealed him inside an iron tank. Houdini took an hour to get out . He also jumped off bridges and freed himself from handcuffs underwater.

At home in his basement shop, he worked on his locks and magic tricks. Often he would work ten or twelve hours without remembering to eat. Then he would drink two quarts of milk into which a dozen eggs had been stirred.

**Houdini, in handcuffs and leg irons, is sealed inside the packing case. The case is dropped in the water. Then Houdini escapes!**

Except for his work, Houdini was forgetful about many things. Often he would run out to the theater wearing one black and one tan sock.

With his money, he was both giving and penny-pinching. When an out-of-work magician wrote to ask him for money, Houdini wrote out a check for $500. Then he scolded his secretary when she tipped over a bottle of ink on the envelope and the ink ran onto the three-cent stamp!

He was as giving with his time as with his money. He never said no when people asked him to give free shows at hospitals, prisons, or old people's homes. He never told reporters about these shows. "When you do a good deed," he told Bess, "you don't take along a brass band."

Part of each day he set aside for exercise to keep his body strong. He used his large bathtub to practice holding his breath for underwater escapes. In winter he poured ice water into the tub to train for a jump into a cold river. He wrote in his notebook:

"Jan. 9. Took cold bath, 49 degrees."

"Jan. 16. Cold bath, 40 degrees. Gee, it's cold."

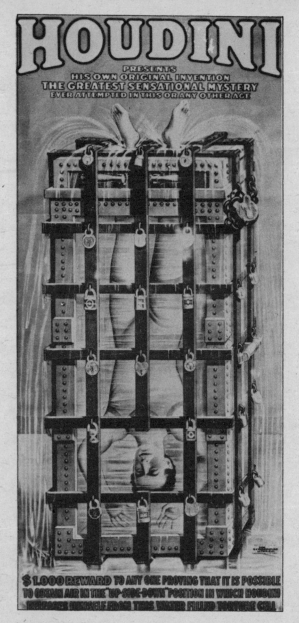

Houdini hung by his heels in this
locked, water-filled cabinet.

"Jan. 18. Taking icy baths to get ready for bridge jump. Water about 36 degrees."

Through training, Houdini was able to hold his breath underwater for four minutes and sixteen seconds!

At the age of 38, he was the best-known magician and escape artist in America. He had all the money he needed. Yet he never forgot the years when he wasn't so famous.

In 1912, at a New York theater, he asked for his weekly pay in $20 gold pieces. "But why?" Bess asked. "You'll see," he replied.

In his dressing room, Harry carefully polished the 50 gold pieces. At home he told Mother Weiss to spread her apron. Into it he poured the coins — $1,000. For a moment, both thought of that evening years before when a young messenger boy had asked his mother to shake him and quarters had poured from his sleeves.

But the next year, tragedy struck his happy life. Mother Weiss died. In his notebook, Houdini wrote: "Everything seemed turned to dust and ashes for me. . . . I was alone with my bitter agony."

To overcome his sorrow, Houdini worked even harder. In July 1914 he introduced a new trick — walking through a brick wall.

A large rug, covered by a sheet, was placed at the center of the stage. As Houdini performed, workmen built a nine-foot brick wall on a wheeled base at the side of the stage. When it was completed, they rolled it onto the sheet, placing it so that the end of the wall faced the audience. Houdini then stepped to the front of the stage and asked for thirty people to come up and watch closely. He had them stand on the edges of the sheet to hold it in place. Now, even if there were a trap door under the wall, there was no way Houdini could get to it.

Stagehands then placed a three-sided screen against each side of the wall. Houdini stepped inside the screen at the left. People on the stage and in the audience saw him wave his hand above it. "Here I am!" he called. A moment later, the screen on the right opened. There he stood, smiling at the surprised audience. He appeared to have gone right through a brick wall!

In addition to his daily shows, Houdini gave special shows to raise money for America's war effort during World War I.

In January 1918 an ad appeared in New York newspapers: "The World Famous Houdini Offers His Latest Creation, The Vanishing Elephant."

The theater was crowded. Houdini stood in the center of the stage. Behind him was a cabinet—as large as a two-car garage. Doors at the rear were open, and a curtain in front was raised. The audience could look right through the cabinet and see that it was empty. An orchestra played soft music.

"Ladies and gentlemen," Houdini said, "may I present — Jennie!"

From the side of the stage walked a five-ton elephant wearing a blue ribbon. Her trainer led her into the cabinet.

Houdini walked to the rear and closed the two doors. Then he pulled a curtain across the front of the cabinet.

He held up his hand, and the band stopped playing. "When I count to three, Jennie will have disappeared!"

He took hold of a corner of the curtain. "One— two — three!" With one motion he whipped back the curtain and stood to one side. The audience could see straight through the cabinet and out a window in the doors at the rear. The cabinet was empty!

When reporters asked Houdini how he could make such a large animal disappear, he smiled. "Even the elephant does not know how it is done."

It was during these years that Houdini again became interested in spiritualism. But this time he didn't want to "talk with spirits." Now he wanted to become a ghost breaker — to show up fake spiritualists who pretended to bring messages from loved ones in the "great beyond."

That is what he told reporters. But Houdini had another interest in spiritualism, one that reporters didn't know about. In showing up fake spiritualists, he was really looking for an honest one, one who *could* talk with spirits.

"Maybe," he told Bess, "just maybe I can get in touch with Mama. I long to hear her lovely voice again."

# 8. The Ghost Breaker

In October 1922 a reporter asked Houdini an important question: "Do you believe it is possible to talk with people who have died?"

Houdini thought for a moment. "My mind is open," he said. He wanted to believe it was possible, for he longed to get a message from his mother. But he had never seen proof that living people could talk with loved ones who had died.

In the 1920s many Americans were asking the same question. Mediums — people who said they could talk with the spirits of dead people — gave seances in most cities in the United States.

Some mediums charged only one dollar or two dollars for a seance. But there were others who charged 100 dollars or more. In one year they made thousands of dollars.

Most seances were alike. People sat around a table in a dark room. The medium led them in prayer, and they sang a hymn, like "In the Sweet Bye and Bye."

Then the medium, holding the hands of people next to him, called the "spirits." A glowing trumpet would rise, float in the darkness, and play a few notes. Ghostly hands appeared and disappeared. The table began to move. A chain rattled. Then ghostly voices passed on messages from dead relatives to the people seated around the table. These voices came from "spirits" with names like Little Rose, Uncle John, Aunt Susan, and Chief Big Elk.

Houdini visited many mediums, trying to find one who could get a message from his mother. He went to one medium who seemed honest. "I was willing to believe, even wanted to believe," he said. "With a beating heart I waited, hoping that I might feel once more the presence of my beloved mother."

But he was disappointed. The medium passed on a message from Mother Weiss. Houdini noted that the message was in English. Mrs. Weiss had not been able to speak or read the language. The day also happened to be his mother's birthday, but the "spirit" didn't mention that.

He sent Bess to other seances. The results were just as false. She received messages from her dead children — the Houdinis never had children. She also received messages from her dead mother. Bess's mother was very much alive.

"The more I look into the subject," Houdini wrote in his notebook, "the less I can make myself believe." Mediums were interested only in taking money from "believers," he told Bess. They had no messages to pass on from dead relatives.

During his stage shows, he began giving talks to audiences on spirit mediums.

He showed how a "hand" could float in a dark room. The medium painted a glove with special paint that glowed in the dark. Then he placed the glove on the end of a long stick. The stick was painted black so no one could see it in the dark. People saw only the glowing "hand."

The floating table was lifted by the medium's foot. His helper, covered by a black sheet so no one

Houdini in one of the
disguises he used
while searching for
a true medium.

could see him, held a "floating" trumpet and played notes.

Mediums began watching for Houdini. If he came to a seance, they refused to go on with it. So Houdini went to one seance wearing a false beard and wig. As a trumpet floated in the darkness, he snapped on a powerful flashlight. There was the medium holding the trumpet to his lips.

Taking off his beard and wig, Houdini cried, "It is I, Houdini! I hereby accuse you of fraud and deception!"

A detective arrested the medium, and reporters waiting outside had another good story.

In September 1925 Houdini offered $10,000 to anyone who could produce a real spirit. But no one tried for the money. Houdini was still secretly hoping to speak with his mother, but deep within himself, he was disappointed. He knew then that he would never talk with his mother again.

**Houdini shows how some "spirit hands" were made in a mold with wax.**

# 9. The Last Act

By 1926 Houdini had become a superstar of magic. The years of study and hard work had made him a master magician.

His show opened with several puzzling tricks. He wrapped a glowing lamp in a silk cloth. When he drew the cloth away, the lamp had disappeared.

Alarm clocks vanished from his hands. They appeared again on the far side of the stage hanging from blue ribbons and clanging loudly.

He showed the audience an empty cabinet. Then he closed the doors, fired a blank pistol, and four girls stepped out.

He hung a cloth over one hand. When he pulled the cloth away, there in his hand was a bowl of live goldfish.

People from the audience came up on stage. They chose five cards from a pack. Houdini tore

Harry Houdini climbed into this water-filled milk can. Six padlocks held the top of the can in place. But Houdini escaped alive!

the cards into bits and stuffed them into a pistol. He fired the gun at a large star across the stage. The same five cards popped up on the points of the star.

In the second half of the show, Houdini escaped from the Chinese water torture—a locked, water-filled cabinet. As the final curtain dropped, he came out to take his bow, dripping wet and tired. The people cheered and clapped.

And then his life suddenly ended.

After an afternoon show at the Princess Theater in Montreal in October 1926, a young man visited Houdini in his dressing room. He was a college boxing star at McGill University.

Houdini was lying on a sofa reading his mail. The young man had admired Houdini's strong body. He asked if he could "throw a punch" at the magician's stomach.

Without looking up, Houdini mumbled "Sure—anytime."

The young boxer swung hard. Houdini dropped the letters and clutched his stomach. The youth

Houdini being lowered head first into the
Chinese Water Torture cabinet.

was surprised. "Hold on," Houdini gasped, his face white. "I have to get set for it."

He stood, set his muscles, and the young man swung again. This time, his fist felt as if it had hit an oak plank.

On the train to Detroit the next day, Houdini's temperature rose to 102 degrees. But he insisted on giving his show for the Sunday night crowd at the Garrick Theater. "They're here to see me," he told Bess. "I won't disappoint them."

After the show, Houdini collapsed and was taken to Grace Hospital. On Monday afternoon the doctors operated on him and removed a torn appendix.

Twice a day the hospital gave out news stories on Houdini's condition. Newspapers across the United States published the stories. By Saturday morning the hospital was saying that his condition was "less than favorable."

On Sunday morning, he whispered to Bess, "I'm tired of fighting.... I guess this thing is going to get me."

On October 31, 1926 — Halloween — Houdini died. He was 52 years old.

Houdini was buried in Brooklyn, New York, in a grave next to his mother's.

Two days before his death, Houdini had told Bess that he would try to reach her from the "other side." "Remember this message," he whispered. " 'Rosabelle, believe.' When you hear those words, you will know that I am speaking to you from beyond the grave."

"Rosabelle" was the title of a song Bess had sung at Coney Island when the Master Monarchs of Modern Mystery had set out on their remarkable life together.

Bess kept a light shining in front of her husband's picture day and night for years. Each Halloween she sat faithfully near the picture and waited. But no message came. On the tenth year after Houdini's death, she turned off the light. "I don't believe he will come," she said.

After a few years, Bess sold the house on 113th Street. Houdini's library of 5,200 books on magic went to the Library of Congress in Washington, D.C. His large collection of tricks, locks, and handcuffs was given to his fellow magicians and friends.

Bess opened a tea room in New York, but soon closed it. She tried her own magic show. Without her husband beside her, she really had no interest in the work. In 1943, on a train in California, she suffered a heart attack. She never recovered.

In time, radio, TV, and movies took the place of stage shows. Now most of the old theaters in which Houdini spent 33 years mystifying people have been torn down.

But the memory of Harry Houdini, the Master Magician, lives on.